This book is filled with terms, reports and everything I
needed for my small business needs.
— Famous person

QUICKBOOKS

Small Business Bookkeeping and Accounting Guide

The Best QuickBooks Guide for Successful Small Businesses

Presented By

The Preneur's Guide

Authored By

Zachary Weiner

Zachary Weiner LLC
157 E. 86th St. #506
New York, NY, 10028
zac@zacweiner.com

ISBN-13: 978-0692957790 (paperback)
ISBN-10: 0692957790 (paperback)

Ordering Information:
Quantity sales. Special discounts are available on quantity purchases by
corporations, associations, and others. For details, contact the publisher
at the address above.

This book is dedicated to the people in my life (you know who you are) that refused to give up on me and my wild dreams.

Contents

Introduction

Business is hard, no question about that. Whether you are a solopreneur, a small business owner, or a large business owner, the challenges are truly endless—from marketing and sales, to HR and financial reporting. Of course, in reality, these challenges come with personal and financial freedoms that cannot be achieved working for someone else. Ask any business owner if they could see themselves working under another owner—an overwhelming amount say no!

This book does not serve as an all-inclusive guide to business and finance. A book of that nature would be endless, as new questions arise daily from various industries. This small book serves instead as a starting guide, a framework for the small business owner to better understand and report their financials using one of the most popular software program currently on the market—QuickBooks.

Software changes rapidly. As I am writing this book, there have already been significant changes in the QuickBooks Online reconciliation feature. Despite these changes, the rationale for QuickBooks-based accounting and the approaches to it described in the pages below will continue to be relevant. Focus on absorbing the large themes, as these will guide you in the direction you hope to take—financial and accounting success.

I personally despise introductions, so let's get into what you came here to read. Over the coming pages, you will be educated on the most popular accounting software with the goal of making endless challenges easier to handle.

Chapter 1

Why Account At All?

Why Account At All?

You may ask yourself why you should account at all: Why do I need to track what is going on in my business? Without understanding and capably navigating accounting terms and reports you won't be able to succeed in the long term. Accounting is the basic framework of a business. I'm sure you have heard of the terms: profit and loss, cost of goods sold, gross profit, return on investment. But these and many other terms may sound foreign and overwhelming. At the end of the year, when your CPA requests your balance sheet, income statement, and statement of cash flows, do you avoid returning the email? For the lucky few of you who have business partners who've invested capital, it becomes even more challenging because you might feel that your partners are talking a different language. Quarterly or monthly investment meetings centered around the language of business just aren't an easy or productive task for a novice. You may not be well-versed in what those terms are and what those reports mean, so to imagine yourself working within QuickBooks seems impossible.

Pause, in the pages below we will cover all those challenging terms and more. More importantly, each term will be explained in plain English so you can make solid financial decisions based on accurate financials. Knowledge of terms will make your business meeting more productive and the ability to make sound financial decisions much more attainable.

Accounting is not a recent development. It has been around since the Romans marked their stone tablets with notches for their number of sheep. In fact, you probably learned all the basic accounting tools necessary for success in grade school.
Understanding the goals of accounting will allow you to better reach your business objectives. Accounting serves two main purposes:

1. To educate you, the business owner, on what is going on in your business
2. To help you report your business operations to the IRS

It's really just that simple.

Let's dive a bit deeper.

Why Educate Yourself?

Why would you want to educate yourself about your business? This may seem like an odd and idiotic question—why would you need to know more about your business, like come on, it's YOUR business? Looking at your business and its goals through the lens of accounting will give you a fresh perspective and allow you to make better decisions. Educating yourself about your business is really the main point of financial reporting. Budgets allow you to set business goals for you and your team. Financial reports allow you to see if you've met the goals you set for yourself. Reporting allows you to highlight points where you fell short or missed the mark. Key performance indicators (KPIs for short) allow you to measure your business against others within your industry to see how you stand.

Through education, you can make better decisions. Better decisions result in a better business. And we all know a better business results in a better life for our family and sounder sleep at night. Instead of thinking about financials as some incomprehensible chicken scratch that only the MBAs can understand, think about it as a mentor to help guide your business to success. Similarly, the time tested accounting principles have led businesses to success for hundreds of years. Today's accounting software is both user-friendly and time effective. These accounting principles will serve as your mentors in helping your business grow or consolidate to ensure that you profit in the best way possible.

Many big questions come to mind for a small business operation: Should I hire another staff member? Do I make money on this product? Should I focus on x part of my business? Should I offer free shipping? Do I charge enough for my product? QuickBooks has these answers hidden within it, and they are there for the taking. The next few chapters will help you pull those answers out.

Thoroughly understanding these financial reports and key metrics will give you the answers you are searching for. Complex questions will be able to be seen in a yes or no format. Key margins can be calculated with simple division, and profitability will be available as a percentage of revenue.

Why Report Your Business?

The IRS and state governments want to know what you do. The state wants to know how many items you sell, if your business made any money, if you personally made money, and how much you paid in taxes. The IRS wants to know how and in what format you made or lost money. Whatever political court you harbor your beliefs, the government requires you to pay taxes, and QuickBooks helps you do just that.

The expression is timeless and truly annoying; "but in this world nothing can be said to be certain, except death and taxes." In America, one cannot get through life without the two. No matter your political affiliation or how you feel about paying your earnings or profit to the government, taxes are unavoidable. The risks greatly outweigh the slight benefits of avoiding paying a small share of your earnings to the government.

By understanding how to correctly track expenses and account for items, such as sales tax, you can ensure you remain compliant and never fear the wrath of the IRS or state governments. By accounting properly for large equipment purchases, leasehold improvement, store build outs, etc., you can ensure you take the proper deductions for years to come. We will touch on the proper accounting procedures for those items later on.

Chapter 2

A Short History Lesson

History of Accounting

Every university offers semester-long lectures on the history of business and/or the history of accounting. In that course, professors lecture about how accounting has been around since things needed to be counted (i.e. when the Romans marked their stone tablets with notches for their number of sheep). Accounting in the form we see it today has been around since states or nations needed to report finances to the king or ruler. The basis of accounting is to report accurate financial information.

Accounting in the form of double entry, the format popular in our current society, was really brought to light in the late fifteenth century by Luca Pacioli. He was the first to document the world of double accounting and much more in a legible written format. To be honest, he changed our interpretation of accounting as we know it and that of algebra (yes, his famous book outlined the basics of algebra, too). As I previously mentioned, the math you learned in grade school is all you need to account properly.

I won't bore you with a semester-long history lesson here, but the fact is that Luca documented the basic accounting principles of today. It was the idea that everything should be accounted for or have an entry. He had a ledger that included assets such as inventory and receivables, liabilities, cash, income, and expenses. He even went so far as to suggest not sleeping if all the numbers did not tie. He was widely considered the father of accounting and even provided year-end closing entries (something today's CPAs regularly supply).

The Story Behind QuickBooks Rise to Fame

Back in the 80s, accounting software was overwhelming and tedious. When you did double entry accounting, you had to do two entries: Hence the term double entry. You had to credit and debit the right accounts and know all the tricks of the trade. For those of you who took that business course back in college—you may remember those miserable debit and credit lectures. (Or more likely you remember the fantastic naps you had at 9:00 a.m. Mondays, Wednesdays, and Fridays.)

During the 80s, Intuit—the makers of QuickBooks—came out with a product that eliminated the need for double entry. Intuit realized that small business owners were busy running their business and not researching the intricacies of double-entry accounting. It took a few different versions before the elite accounting world accepted the product, but it quickly grew to over 80 percent market share of the accounting software for small businesses.

QuickBooks made accounting software more approachable and user-friendly. It allowed business owners to take control of their businesses and has empowered these small business owners ever since. Simultaneous with the rise of tools for small business

was growth in small business and solo
entrepreneurship.

QuickBooks and other Intuit software programs are
designed to make your business life easier. Think of
QuickBooks as a tool, like your email or your
smartphone, that allows you to connect with
customers, employees, partners, and business
owners all over the world and that helps you solve
problems all hours of the day.

Chapter 3

The Language of Accounting

Why all these funny words?

Oftentimes industry professionals develop their own language. Initially the idea behind this was likely to communicate better with their peers. But it has turned into a barrier to entry—confusing terms and analogies with the goal of keeping outsiders out.

Do you need to pay a professional $500 or more an hour if you can figure out the answers to the questions yourself? No, you do not need a high-level professional for much of what is going on in your business. You just need to better understand the terms and the associated ideas behind those.

The List!

Accounts Payable

Accounts payable (A/P) is the amount a business owes its suppliers or creditors. Oftentimes these are debts that must be paid off within a given period to avoid default. On many company's balance sheets, accounts payable is often logged as a current liability.

The payable is essentially a short-term IOU from the business to the other business, who acts as a creditor.

Accounts Receivable

Accounts receivable (A/R) is the amount a business is owed by its customers. This number fluctuates over the course of the business and should be reviewed often. On your company's balance sheet, accounts receivable is often logged as an asset.

Accrual Basis Accounting

Accrual Basis Accounting refers to one of the two major accounting methods. Accrual Basis Accounting is a method that records revenues and expenses when they are incurred, regardless of when cash is received or disbursed. The term accrual refers to any individual entry recording revenue or expense in the absence of a cash transaction. One example of this would be invoicing a customer but not yet receiving payment—the invoice is recorded as revenue but the cash transaction has yet to occur. Another example would be entering an invoice before payment has been remitted.

Asset

Any resource of economic value that a company owns. Yes, your truck is an asset if owned by the company. The money you used to build out the fixtures and furnishing in your store is an asset. The computer equipment that sits on your desk is an asset. So on and so forth.

Balance Sheet

A company's balance sheet gives a snapshot of the company's financial health in a given moment. This includes the cash it has on hand, bank account balances, the liabilities it has outstanding, and equity the owners have in the business.

Bottom Line

This is the total amount a business has made or lost at the end of a given period. The reference to bottom describes the relative location of the net income on a company's income statement. The term can also be used in the context of a business's earnings increasing or decreasing.

Cash Basis Accounting

Cash basis refers to the other major accounting method. This approach recognizes revenues and expenses at the time physical cash is actually received or paid out. When transactions are recorded on a cash basis, they affect a company's books only once a completed exchange of value has occurred; therefore, cash basis accounting is less accurate than accrual accounting in the short term.

Cash Flow

This is usually defined by investors as being the key metric to a firm's financial health. Cash flow is really the difference between what you report on your financial statements that is not cash and cash transactions that actually occur.

In the accrual method of accounting, you are allowed to count your chickens before they hatch. This means that you can record money coming in and expenses leaving before the physical cash transaction actually occurs. For example, when you create an invoice, the sale has occurred, but really do you have the money yet? No! Cash flow reverses out all these items and gives you a true understanding of your real dollars in hand.

This is oftentimes displayed in a statement of cash flows.

Debt

Similar to your house mortgage, a debt is money owed on an asset. A debt in business could mean a loan, a line of credit, or money you borrowed from your mother. Better keep these debts in check to make sure your business stays healthy.

Depreciation

Large expenditures, such as the purchase of a vehicle or building, will add value to the business over an extended period. Accounting treats these purchases differently and will make them an expense over their usable life. For example, a vehicle will likely serve your business for seven years, so you will take an annual expense for this vehicle over seven years. Over time, a business' assets decrease in value due to the time that has passed since it was purchased. For tax purposes, a business can recover the cost of that depreciation through a deduction. Consult with your CPA to set a depreciation schedule and ensure you are depreciating all your assets correctly.

Expenses

Business expenses are the costs the company incurs in order to operate. These are such things as rent, utilities, professional and legal fees, employee wages, contractor pay, and marketing and advertising costs.

Liability

This is simply an obligation to repay debt. Oftentimes this is similar to a loan or line of credit. But a liability goes a bit farther and can be sales tax you owe the government or payroll taxes you owe the state.

Net Income

In the most basic sense, this means a company's total earnings or profit. You start with income, money from the sales of services or goods. You minus out COGS, an expense for creating the previously mentioned sales or good. Then, you minus out everything else you spent money on—such as gas for the truck, a manager to run the store, etc. All that is left (which I hope for your sake is a lot) is your net income. P.S. an increase in net income is usually a good thing!

Net Worth

Assets minus liability, used by both companies and individuals. A continual increase in net worth indicates good financial health; conversely, net worth may be depleted by business losses.

Profit and Loss (income statement)

Also known as a profit and loss statement, an income statement shows the profitability of a business during a period of time. The income statement looks at a business' revenues, cost of goods, and expenses through all of its activities (including all bank accounts, credit cards, etc.).

Chapter 4

Which QuickBooks is Right for You?

QuickBooks for Mac

Who's it for?
This is a bit obvious, but this product is for Mac users. With the many keyboard tricks integrated into the Mac operating system, QuickBooks for Mac enables the user to reach optimum efficiency.

Where does it live?
The QuickBooks files and applications live on your Mac. The company file can be stored on an external hard drive, but to ensure that you do not corrupt the file, it is best to have this stored on your Mac.

What features are included?
All the features you would expect from a desktop version of QuickBooks are included. For an extra fee, the file can be hosted in the cloud, allowing access from a multiple Mac computers located at different locations.

What features are forgotten?
Cloud hosting and automatic updates are not included in the version for Mac desktops. Additionally, you are limited to access by only three users, so it has potential to limit you as you grow your small business.

What's it cost?
The real cost of the software is $299 per year, but it also requires an annual support contract of $299 that recurs yearly.

Is it user-friendly?
What is great about the Mac for QuickBooks is that it is built for Macs. QuickBooks for Macs make use of Mac keyboard shortcuts, and as an avid Mac user myself, I know that keyboard shortcuts save time (and thus money)!

What else do you need to know about this software?
Of all of the desktop versions of QuickBooks, the Mac version is the least robust. As your business grows and you need a more advanced version of QuickBooks, you will be all but forced to move to the PC version. QuickBooks Pro, QuickBooks Premier, and QuickBooks Enterprise are PC-based systems, so it may be best to focus your energies on setting yourself up the right way from the get-go to save you headaches down the line.

Final Thoughts
This product is for a Mac addict. If you can live without your Mac, go with one of the other versions listed below.

QuickBooks Online

Who's it for?
QuickBooks Online is designed for anyone to access. You can access the same file from a PC, Mac, or even from your smartphone (yes, you can even code your bank feed from your smartphone). Simply put, QuickBooks Online allows access from all your computer devices.

Where does it live?
The file lives in the world of Intuit (the QuickBooks parent company). It is likely on an Amazon server either in Virginia or Northern California, depending on your location. In layman's terms, it lives in the cloud.

What features are included?
All of the basic QuickBooks features are included. This ranges from customers, journal entries, bank feeds, bank reconciliations, and so on. Some of the more advanced features that Pro, Premier, and Enterprise users might expect are not included.

What features are forgotten?
All of the robust find features, advanced sorting features, and a lot of other features considered the norm for the desktop products are missing. Business owners who have used the desktop products for years often find the transition to QBO very difficult.

What's it cost?

The online version is comparable to the desktop versions. It starts at $20 per month, which comes out to about $240 annually. If you prefer more features, such as the ability to send estimates, have multiple users, and track inventory—the price will increase.

Is it user-friendly?

QuickBooks Online is like all software-as-a-service products you would experience in today's world. A software-as-a-service product is an application, like one on your smart phone, where both the software and the data are provided to a customer for a reoccurring fee. The user interface is friendly and fairly simple. Overall, the software is simpler and easier to navigate from the start.

What else do you need to know about this software?

This QuickBooks Online software is really designed for a small business owner just starting out. If you have one stream of revenue, a few bills, and a small list of expenses, this is the perfect software for you. It also allows for you to pay monthly versus a larger upfront fee.

Final Thoughts

QuickBooks Online is very solid small business accounting software. If this is your first foray into small business accounting, it will give you all you need. If you have multiple profit centers, need complex invoicing, and plan on having a few staff members in your accounting departments—the products to follow are best for you.

QuickBooks Pro

Who's it for?
QuickBooks Desktop Pro is the most basic of the PC versions of QuickBooks Desktop. This is accounting software focused on small businesses for those that use a PC.

Where does it live?
The file can live on your desktop, on a server, or in the cloud. The cloud storage has an additional cost associated with it.

What features are included?
All the basic features you would expect from accounting software are included. You can enter customers, vendors, perform journal entries, reconciliations, and so on.

What features are forgotten?
The main features missing in QuickBooks Pro are the ability perform business specific reports, create and manage budgets, and tracking 1099 contractors. Additionally the inventory features are not as advanced as the higher versions of QuickBooks and could be challenging if you have a complex product that you resell.

What's it cost?

QuickBooks Pro costs an initial fee of $299. The annual subscription runs the same price. Hosting through QuickBooks also has additional costs associated with it.

Is it user-friendly?

Desktop versions of QuickBooks are moderately user-friendly. Out of the box, there are a vast number of decisions the designated administrator must make, and initially this can be overwhelming. However, there are a handful of PC keyboard tricks that make it very user-friendly for PC addicts.

What else do you need to know about this software?

The QuickBooks Pro software is really designed for a small business owner who prefers desktop software and is just starting out. The Pro version is great for one stream of revenue, a few bills, and a small list of expenses. It is also great as you grow your staff and add complexity to your accounting.

Final Thoughts

Overall, QuickBooks Pro is solid software focused on your current and future small business needs. It's a cost-effective solution for a very small team with fewer than three users and no need for creating and emailing sales orders. Initially the software is a bit overwhelming, but this book makes it less intimidating.

Pro Tip
Pro Tip
Once your QuickBooks Pro file is generated, you can always upgrade to Premier or Enterprise.

QuickBooks Premier

Who's it for?
QuickBooks Premier is a more advanced version of QuickBooks Desktop. This is accounting software focused on small businesses that are growing and have expanding needs. Additionally, this is for users who prefer to use a PC-based software.

Where does it live?
The file can live on your desktop, on a server, or in the cloud. The cloud storage has an additional cost associated with it.

What features are included?
All the basic features you would expect from accounting software are included, plus much more. You can enter customers, vendors, perform journal entries, reconciliations, and so on. Additionally QuickBooks Premier offers 50+ additional reporting options above QuickBooks Pro. You also have the ability to have up to five users work simultaneously.

What features are forgotten?
QuickBooks Premier is very robust and covers most of the features needed to successfully account for your small business. The items that are forgotten are complex reporting and tracking features for small businesses that are scaling—these solutions can only be found in QuickBooks Enterprise.

What's it cost?
QuickBooks Premier is $499 for a one-time software fee. The annual subscription is required and runs the same price every year after that. Hosting through QuickBooks also has additional costs associated with it.

Is it user-friendly?
Desktop versions of QuickBooks are moderately user-friendly. Out of the box, there are a vast number of decisions the designated administrator must make, and initially this can be overwhelming. However, there are a handful of PC keyboard tricks that make it very user-friendly for PC addicts.

What else do you need to know about this software?
QuickBooks Premier is really designed for a small business owner who prefers desktop software and is past the basic phase of their business. Premier is great for multiple streams of revenue, many bills, and any number of expenses. It is also robust and designed for an accounting team of five.

Final Thoughts

Overall, QuickBooks Premier is solid software focused on the needs of your growing small business now and in the future. It's a cost-effective solution that is great for smaller teams of up to five users. Initially the software is a bit overwhelming, but this book makes it less so.

QuickBooks Enterprise

Who's it for?

QuickBooks Enterprise is the most advanced version of QuickBooks on the market. This product's core consumer is a complex small to mid-size business with multiple individuals in the accounting department.

Where does it live?

This product could live on your corporate server or in the Intuit cloud.

What features are included?

All the basic QuickBooks features are included and much more. Ever think you would like to track 1 million customers? Need 30 staff members working in QuickBooks at once? Need consolidated financial reports? QuickBooks Enterprise does all those things and has features built in to do even more.

What features are forgotten?
In terms of QuickBooks, no features are forgotten.
However, if you are considering QuickBooks
Enterprise, you need to take a deep look at your
firm's needs. QuickBooks Enterprise is robust
software, but it is not nearly as robust as financial
enterprise resource planning (ERP) software on the
market.

What's it cost?
Depending on if hosting is included and how many
users need access, the product price can range from
$150 to $1,000 per month. Yes, you are talking about
real robust accounting needs, and the price reflects
that.

Is it user-friendly?
The more basic features of QuickBooks Enterprise
are similar to that of other QuickBooks products.
They are easy to use and easy to learn. The more
complex features of Enterprise can be challenging
and take some time to learn for an untrained
accountant.

What else do you need to know about this software?
QuickBooks Enterprise is a robust software and the
most advanced version of Intuit's QuickBooks
product lines. This software is for expanding
businesses that are outgrowing all the other basic
products and need to manage lots of data or need to
report on multiple entities. This is the most advanced

QuickBooks software before transitioning to a truly custom accounting software such as an ERP.

A Quick Aside

For those of you who operate or plan on operating different entities (for example, you have an LLC for your digital products, an LLC for your brick and mortar retail, an S Corp for your management firm, etc.) you will need to understand the costs associated with choosing a version of QuickBooks software. The online version of QuickBooks charges you on a per-entity basis. So the key takeaway is that if you plan to manage multiple legal entities with QuickBooks, you really should look long and hard at the versions of QuickBooks Desktop before taking the leap with QuickBooks Online.

Chapter 5

Charting Your Accounts, AKA the Chart of Accounts

What Is a Chart of Accounts?

Merriam Webster defines a chart of accounts as a *list of account names arranged systematically and usually coded numerically or alphabetically or both to form the general framework of the accounting system of a specific business and to establish a scheme of account classification.*

In layman's terms, the chart of accounts is a list of expenses or incomes that have numbers associated with them. These items are used to prepare financial statements. It really is that simple: a chart of accounts is a list of items used to help you prepare better financial statements. There is some method behind the madness of the crazy numbering, subaccounts, and other complexities. But the chart of accounts in QuickBooks is simply a framework to make accounting easier.

Why Is Accounting like Building a Home?

To first understand the need for a chart of accounts in QuickBooks, you must first understand how a home is constructed. A house begins as a thought. This mental process often begins before construction or land purchase. It starts off as a family's desire to have a place where they can share their memories. Your business begins the same way. It's an idea, a thought—one that could transform your life and give you the freedom to make your own path.

The next step in the process, once you get serious about building a home, is acquiring the land necessary to build the home. In the world of business ownership and accounting, QuickBooks is like the land the house is built on. It is where the business is will be built—where the chart of accounts will be set up. If the land is where your home lives, then you can think of QuickBooks as the place where your business information lives. Just as land turns the idea of a home into a reality, your purchase of QuickBooks turns your business ideas into success.

The next step in homebuilding is often reaching out to an architect and developing plans. This equates to developing the chart of accounts. To better set up QuickBooks, you will use the chart of accounts provided below and modify it for your particular needs. This would be like buying a home in a neighborhood where the developer has a few different home models but we can modify the home finishes.

Once the home is built to specification, or once you have set up QuickBooks and the chart of accounts, including bank accounts, importing first expenses, billing clients/entering sales, it is ready to "inhabit." The early tasks may initially seem tedious, but working through them ensures your business is in as tidy an order as a house that has been carefully and efficiently unpacked.

Running your business is like living in your home. A business needs constant upkeep and cleaning. It also needs maintenance, such as cleaning, repair, a new roof, pressure washing, etc. QuickBooks and your chart of accounts may expand or contract. You may add a room to your house, and similarly in business, you add new accounts. You may realize that you no longer need an extra bedroom and just use it for storage, perhaps even downsizing your home or comparably removing items from your chart of accounts.

Why Are the Chart of Accounts So Important?

Oftentimes we hear people harp on the importance of one item or another. You must do this or do that to be successful. A majority of you have heard this and followed your own path, but the chart of accounts is truly important, so don't skim the next few pages.

The reality of a good chart of accounts is that it makes your life easier in both a business analysis and a tax reporting context. Let's say you run a complex retail business and have both salespeople on the floor, management managing those people, production employees, and their managers. Yes, all of the above items are payroll expenses for your small firm, but business decisions cannot be made by looking at that number in total. The chart of accounts helps to break up this number. By breaking it up into departments and even roles (such as management versus non-management), you will be able to see on a weekly, monthly, quarterly, and yearly basis how productive your team is, how much revenue was created by payroll expenses, and how much product was added to inventory by payroll expenses.

Let's take this example a step further. By focusing on the week-over-week expense for these departments and roles, you should be able to establish a minimum operating expense and, respectively, a quality operating percentage for when the business gets busy. More salesmen and women are obviously necessary as business picks up, but it is more valuable to make some customers wait 5 minutes than lose money on a given day. By extrapolating those numbers with an in-depth chart of accounts from which you can run actual reports, you will be able to make better business decisions.

A well-established chart of accounts in QuickBooks helps you run your business better. How much are you spending on client meals? How much is your payroll costing you? How many refunds did you have last week? All these answers can be pulled from a quality chart of accounts, so pay attention!

Example of a Chart of Accounts

QuickBooks comes preloaded with a few different chart of account templates. You will be asked what industry you operate within, and then you will be given a preset chart of accounts. The offerings may have too few or too many accounts and subaccounts, on the other hand, it may have too few. So feel free to use the chart of accounts provided.

Below we will give you an in-depth background on the QuickBooks chart of accounts, their categories, and the associated items with each category. This will lead you down the path of generating the best chart of accounts for your business. Let's be real, at the end of the day, the chart of accounts in QuickBooks is here to serve you.

What Is the Idea Behind the Chart of Accounts Structure?

The chart of accounts is designed to help you organize your business income and expenses. An extension of a chart of accounts is a profit and loss statement. A profit and loss statement (otherwise known as an income statement) shows the profitability of a business during a period of time. It is much more useful to a business operator when it does not break everything down into tiny little bits such as accounts, subaccounts, sub-sub-accounts. The most useful profit and loss statement fits onto just a page or two, don't let this turn into a five-page report. If you want to get detailed information on certain accounts that is what all the robust reporting features inside QuickBooks are built for.

How Do I Standardize My Chart of Accounts (and Make Sure I Make My CPA Happy)?

I hear it all the time: How do I standardize my chart of accounts or make the chart of account comply with Generally Accepted Accounting Principles? Below highlights some of the more standard procedures, but remember one of the major goals of accounting is to serve the business owner's needs—so make your chart of accounts work for you.

A standard chart of accounts is organized according to a numerical system. Remember when you learned to count to 10 as a child? We are just going to relearn how to do that, but this time each number is going to mean something different.

Each major category begins with a certain number, and then the subcategories within that major category all begin with the same number. For example, if assets are classified by numbers starting with the digit 1, then cash accounts might be labeled

1001, accounts receivable might be labeled 1002, inventory might be labeled 1003, and so on. If liabilities accounts are classified by numbers starting with the digit 2, then accounts payable might be labeled 2001, short-term debt might be labeled 2002, and so on.

Depending on the size and complexity of your company, the chart of accounts may include a few dozen accounts or it may include a hundred (super complex businesses can have thousands).

Below is a quick cheat sheet to help you structure your chart of accounts.

1000 – 1999 Assets
2000 – 2999 Liabilities
3000 – 3999 Equity
4000 – 4999 Income or Revenue
5000 – 5999 Cost of Goods Sold
6000 – 6999 Expenses
7000 – 7999 Other Income
8000 – 8999 Other Expenses

What Do You Mean the Chart of Accounts Has Categories?

At this point you may be in information overload mode—overwhelmed. Don't fret—it is not as complicated as you think, especially in QuickBooks. You may have heard some of the terms above or not.

We will dive into each one in a simple format to help you better understand them.

Assets: 1000 – 1999

These are items that your company owns. For example, you could own the money in your bank account or own the computer you are reading this book on. This is usually divided into two categories, and QuickBooks helps you divide it. These categories are current assets and fixed assets.

Current assets are items that can quickly be turned into cash, such as the money in your bank account. (Of course, even though you can put your car on Craigslist and quickly sell the clunker, it is not considered a current asset.) Some other items that may be current assets are savings accounts, money market accounts, accounts receivable, and inventory.

Fixed assets are items you would usually have to sell to generate cash. The minimum amount for fixed assets is often $500. Some examples of these items are that clunker mentioned above, machinery, equipment, computer, cars and so on.

Liabilities: 2000 – 2999

Liabilities are the money your company owes other people. Did you borrow $1,000 from your buddy to cover payroll on that week sales were slow? Well that would be a liability for your entity. Do you collect sales tax that you need to remit to the government? That is a liability because you owe that money, and it is not yours.

Equity: 3000 – 3999

These accounts really depend on how your entity is structured, and they vary depending on if your entity is a sole proprietorship (single member LLC), partnership (multiple member LLC), or corporation.

In QuickBooks, if your entity is a sole proprietorship, you need a Capital account and an Owner's Draw account. The Capital account is to keep track of just that, the total capital (or amount of money) you have invested since starting the business, plus or minus the net profit or loss each year since you started the business. Use the Owner's Draw account for money you take out of the business for personal use, such as paying your car note or Xbox for little Jimmy, cash withdrawals, your distributions, and any money that gets deposited into your personal accounts.

> **Pro Tip**
>
> Note that as a sole proprietor (single member LLC) you do not pay yourself as a regular employee via W-2. You need to distribute and pay taxes on that money. Consult with your CPA to ensure you are following the correct protocol.

If your company is a partnership (think multimember LLC) or Limited Liability Partnership (LLP), you need to set up Capital and Draw accounts for each partner in QuickBooks. For example, Uncle Todd gave you some money to start your business and your wife's dad Joe also kicked in some cash. They would need QuickBooks accounts titled Uncle Todd's Capital and Uncle Todd's Draw. Similarly, Joe would need Wife's Dad Joe Capital and Wife's Dad Joe Draw. As an aside, the money contributed to open the business goes into the Capital account and the money distributed is coded to Draw.

If your company is an S or C corporation or an LLC corporation (different from an LLC partnership), it should have a Common Stock account and sometimes a Preferred Stock account. Common Stock and Preferred Stock represent the total sum of stock the company has issued. An LLC might have Member stock if there is more than one person who owns stock. This is a bit more on the complex level and you should refer to your CPA to ensure you set up these accounts correctly based on your entity type and member structure.

Income or Revenue: 4000 – 4999

Income or revenue is the income your business gets from day-to-day business operations. These include, but are not limited to consulting fees, income for services rendered, reimbursable expenses, or products you sell. Structuring these accounts in QuickBooks is really up to you. Perhaps you run two different departments for your business, then you may want to separate them into subaccounts of income. Or maybe you sell multiple types of products in each department, then you may want sub-sub-accounts. Either way, it's best to remember that less is more.

Oftentimes, refunds and exchanges live in this category. This ensures that your next profit is truly your next profit. Your top line revenue number should be the money you received for the period, not the money received before refunds and item comps.

Cost of Goods Sold (A.K.A. COGS): 5000 – 5999

In QuickBooks, the Cost of Goods Sold includes the cost of raw materials, freight charges for getting raw material to a warehouse, labor for building the finished goods, and freight charges for getting the goods to the customer. For manufacturing businesses, the Cost of Goods Sold includes the costs incurred in producing or building a product. For a wholesale business, Cost of Goods Sold includes the costs of the goods you purchase for resale. For a distributor business, Cost of Goods Sold includes the costs to purchase and distribute goods to the customer. These costs tend to increase as you sell more products or services. If you sold no goods or services, this account should not incur any expenses.

Let's look at the restaurant business as an example. The restaurant's main inputs are the food bought to produce the dishes on the menu. Some operators prefer to see one lump sum of purchases while other choose to break it out into their main inputs of meat, dairy, baked goods, and dry goods. Be creative, figure out what will make your business function better, set guidelines, and follow them.

Expenses: 6000 – 6999

Expenses are the fixed costs that exist even if you sell no products or services. Examples include rent, telephone, insurance, vehicle expense, advertising, and utilities.

Other Income: 7000 – 7999

Other Income in QuickBooks is income you earn outside the normal way you do business, including interest income, gain on the sale of an asset, insurance settlement, a stock sale, or rents from buildings you own when real estate is not your main business focus.

It is likely that you will not use this income type very often.

Other Expenses: 8000 – 8999

Other Expenses refer to an expense that is outside of your normal business, such as a loss on the sale of an asset, or stockbroker fees (though it is not limited to these items and also often includes depreciation, amortization, R&D expenses, finance cost, and income tax expense).

What is the General Ledger?

For all general purposes, the chart of accounts in QuickBooks is very similar to the general ledger. To be more precise, the general ledger is the numbered accounts based off the chart of accounts and stores all the financial transactions for the life of your firm. A general ledger account is an account or record used to sort and store balance sheet and income statement transactions. Examples of general ledger accounts include everything from cash and bank accounts to salary expense and revenue.

Let's say you wanted to see what has gone on in your firm over the past six months. Well, obviously you sit in the office or garage if you are the next Apple and see what is going on in your business. More importantly, you want to see what your company is spending your hard-earned money on, so you use QuickBooks to run the General Ledger report.

This report shows all the transactions that took place within your business and to what codes these items were classified. It really paints a picture of what is going on in your firm, answering questions such as, *why are my advertising expenses so high for the year*? and, *what is going on with my payroll*? Running the General Ledger report for a large period lets you see the fluctuations of certain expenses over a period. For example, has your weekly payroll run doubled? Did the new staff result in a hit in profitability? Did your daily sales revenue decline in the summer time?

Taking a look at your general ledger lets you get very granular about your business and what is going on within it. Reviewing this report also ensures your staff or you have been recording transactions properly. Are all your credit card fees in the right place? Or, do you have all your payroll in the 'Legal and Professional Fees' category and legal and professional fees in the 'Payroll Expense' category?

Pro Tip

Make sure your general ledger is in order now! This makes the closing of the year and preparing of your tax returns a breeze come March. Remember, plan for success, or don't plan and fail.

What Does a Sample Chart of Accounts Look Like?

Account #	Account Name	Type
1010	Checking Account	Bank
1020	Savings Account	Bank
1030	Cash on Hand	Bank
1100	Accounts Receivable	Accounts Receivable
1200	Inventory Asset	Other Current Asset
1400	Prepaid Expenses	Other Current Asset
1410	Processor 1 Receivable	Other Current Asset
1420	Processor 2 Receivable	Other Current Asset
1430	Processor 3 Receivable	Other Current Asset
1440	Employee Cash Advances	Other Current Asset
1500	Furniture and Fixtures	Fixed Asset
1510	Machinery and Equipment	Fixed Asset

1520	Vehicles	Fixed Asset
1530	Other Fixed Assets	Fixed Asset
1540	Leasehold Improvements	Fixed Asset
1700	Accumulated Depreciation	Fixed Asset
1900	Security Deposit Asset	Other Asset
1910	Organizational Cost	Other Asset
1920	Accumulated Amortization	Other Asset
2000	Accounts Payable	Accounts Payable
2300	Sales Tax Payable	Other Current Liabilities
2350	Federal Income Tax Payable	Other Current Liabilities
2700	Notes Payable	Other Current Liabilities
2800	Bank Loan	Long Term Liabilities
3000	Opening Balance Equity	Equity
3100	Partner Contributions	Equity
3200	Partner Distributions	Equity
4100	Sale of Product Income	Income
4200	Refunds	Income
4300	Discounts	Income
4400	Other Primary Income	Income
5100	Cost of Goods Sold	Cost of Goods Sold
5200	Supplies and Materials	Cost of Goods Sold
5300	Change in Inventory	Cost of Goods Sold
6000	Advertising and Promotion	Expense

6050	Auto Expense	Expense
6100	Bank Fees	Expense
6110	Bank Fees (Sub)	Expense
6120	Credit Card Fees	Expense
6150	Charitable Contributions Expense	Expense
6200	Dues and Subscriptions	Expense
6250	Research and Development	Expense
6300	Shipping Expense	Expense
6350	Gift Expense	Expense
6400	Insurance Expense	Expense
6450	Interest Expense	Expense
6500	Legal & Professional Fees	Expense
6510	Accounting Fees (Sub)	Expense
6520	Legal Fees (Sub)	Expense
6530	Professional Fees (Sub)	Expense
6600	License Expense	Expense
6650	Meals and Entertainment	Expense
6700	Office Expense	Expense
6750	Penalties and Fines	Expense
6800	Rent Expense	Expense
6850	Repair and Maintenance	Expense
6900	Salaries and Wages	Expense
6950	Payroll Fees	Expense

6990	Ask My Accountant	Expense
8100	Tax Expense	Other Expense
8200	Bad Debt	Other Expense
8300	Amortization Expense	Other Expense
8400	Depreciation Expense	Other Expense
9000	Gain on Sales of Asset	Other Income

Pro Tip

The above chart of accounts is merely a guide. You need to make adjustments to fit your business and industry. For example, do you have multiple payroll departments? Break them out in subcategories under Salaries and Wages. Do you have multiple profit centers? Break them out in the 4000's. Do you pay rent on both a warehouse and office space? Create subcategories for these items so you can see which expense created which revenue. Are you spending too much on shipping and warehousing? The chart of account should help you figure this out.

Chapter 6

Automate Your Accounting World

How to Make Technology Work For You

Earlier we learned the benefits of fantastic software that does not require double entries for every one transaction. The benefits of technology do not stop there. With the advent of computer apps like QBO, many companies have generated software that allows apps to communicate with each other.

The below is a simplified example of the conversation your apps can have with each other. Of course, this communication takes place in code and happens instantaneously.

> *Internet Point of Sale: Hi, QuickBooks Online, yesterday, Monday the March 21st 2017, we sold $595 on your website yesterday.*

> *QuickBooks Online: Okay great, we will add these sales to the system, can you give me detail on the transactions?*

> *Internet Point of Sale: Sure, $495 was from credit cards and $100 was from PayPal.*

Automation can come in many forms. The overall idea is to make the accounting easier requiring fewer man hours. There are many platforms and software programs that can help you with this process. For those not using QBO there are also other ways to import sales or automate your sales that require some work on your behalf but that save hours of manual entry.

Automate Today, Tomorrow, and Next Month

Technology is often seen as a challenge, similar to how one sees QuickBooks when logging in for the first time. As stated earlier, QuickBooks is a tool to accomplish your goals, and so is technology as a whole.

The benefits of automation run deep. For a small business with annual sales of roughly $1 million USD, it could require up to one business day a week to enter all the sales data necessary to keep sales up to date. The annual cost of this part-time data entry position could easily exceed $10,000. The costs can add up quickly.

When you begin to automate parts of your accounting world, the world of financial reporting becomes easier. The complex sales data you need is already available and in the correct formats. The general ledger accounts are debited and credited correctly. The reports based on certain period dates are correct. The decisions you make based upon your business are correct. All of these equate to your business being on track.

Applications and QuickBooks

There are plenty of apps options currently on the market to help you automate your accounting. We will look at the some of the top players currently in the space and the import/export feature that will never be outdated.

App Connectors

Some of the most popular technology right now is in the form of services that connect multiple apps. For example, your Instagram can talk to an Excel file or your CRM can talk to QuickBooks.

Personally, I have had a lot of success with software that serves as connector. It tracks communication clearly, notifies you of any issues, and—most importantly—keeps accurate data.

In terms of QuickBooks, the ability to pull data from multiple sources is a blessing. You could pull information from your CRM to your payment processors. If you can use the features—go ahead—but make sure you set them up properly!

Exporting From Your Point of Sale

Many older points of sale (POS) offer a feature where you can export the data to both QuickBooks Desktop and QBO. If you properly close out your days in your POS, denoting cash over or short, which checks have been deposited, and which credit cards have been processed, all this data can be imported to save the time of manual entry. This simple file import is a true blessing.

Oftentimes this feature is covered in the onboarding process with your POS. This is considered a classic feature where you would import an IIF or an XML file. Having been around for quite some time, this approach has been perfected.

Having used features like this at large organizations, I have found it beneficial in terms of time savings and accuracy. Adjustments can be made after the fact. The data is imported in a simple fashion and the after-the-fact adjustments can simply be made on the daily entry where it is needed.

Overall, you should really consider how your POS will interact with your accounting software as part of your search for the right solution. Not only does it need to interface well with your staff and the customer, but you need it to serve as a financial tool for you. If you can't get accurate reports or data, how will your business ever succeed?

Auto-Importing Features

Lots of points of sale offer QBO integration features. Initially these seem like a great option: automate your business and save money. Of course that's the goal, but it must be done correctly. Let's dive in a bit further.

When dealing with complex daily sales and revenue being deposited through multiple transaction types (credit card processors, revenue centers) you need to properly track these to reconcile your books correctly. An example of multiple transaction types for credit card processors would be the following: Visa, MasterCard, Amex, cash, and gift card. These transaction types should be deposited into different clearing accounts within your balance sheet. As we discuss later, how else would you verify all the deposits are there? By putting them in separate clearing accounts, you can reconcile accounts to ensure all your money is there. The challenge with many of the points of sale that automate this process is that they offer one solution for all your transactions.

These points of sale will essentially create a pretend bank and deposit all your invoices into that account. These deposits do not actually occur so they will not match actual bank deposits. Oftentimes there are refunds or processing fees that need to be added after the fact. This is 100 percent the incorrect way to process these transactions. There are two reasons why: One, the deposit has not been differentiated based on processor or transaction type. Two, all that data is really not necessary for QuickBooks. If you have it in your POS and have recorded the records, you are fine.

To ensure you are booking sales properly, you need to understand how the POS is importing data. If it splits the data by revenue and transaction types in a nice journal entry, then this is correct. If it brings in each individual invoice and does not allow for you to break out by revenue type and transaction type with nowhere to book your credit card fees, then stay away!

The main difference between this and the auto-importing I will discuss shortly is that exporting from your POS will bring in the total amounts for the day as opposed to individual sales receipts or invoices. This makes dealing with your books much easier and managing the sales if there is a reconciliation issue a breeze.

Overall Thoughts on Automation

Automation at its core is fantastic, it saves time and makes your life simpler. Unfortunately not all the apps or POS features in the market function at the level necessary for your accounting success. In other words, all integrations are not created equal.

Take your time and research your options. You may even want to perform a small sales test prior to committing to a full on integration. See if setting up the data to automatically import works for your case. If not, then you may just be stuck doing the sales entries by hand for some time. Don't fret though, you are not alone in that!

QBO App Store

The QBO App Store is a great place and the home to many integrations to save you time and money. Ever wanted to import the customer information from your CRM into QuickBooks to better invoice clients? You can do that. Ever wanted to import employee time tracking to better pay employees on a weekly basis? You can do that. It does not stop there, plenty of integrations exist.

The key to setting up a good integration is to read the reviews. See how other users are experiencing these apps. Like any app marketplace there are good and bad eggs. See how the product is working for other people in your space, and you can always try the data on a single day or a single batch of information. So, in a worst-case scenario, you can easily delete the information to undo what you incorrectly imported.

Chapter 7

Set A Weekly Schedule

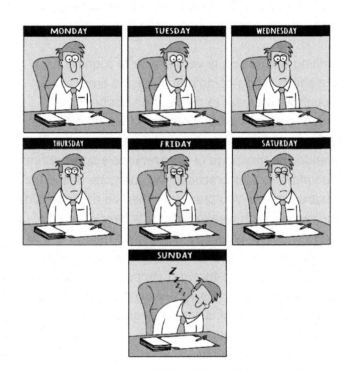

Why Get Organized?

Organization for some comes with ease. For others, it's a daunting nightmare. Are you the former or the latter? If you are the former—skim the following pages. If you are the latter—read three times.

Running a business is very similar to running a household. If you do not set aside the time throughout the year to clean or do not bring in someone else to clean, your home will be disgusting by the end of the year. If you do not have a family calendar on the fridge or on everyone's smartphone, appointments and practices will surely be missed. If you are like me, you create a schedule and set aside time every fourth weekend to do a deep cleaning, and every other weekend do a light cleaning. If you are like me, you have a calendar shared on your smartphone and an itemized shopping list shared in a sharing software. It is very likely that you are not like me yet, and that is why I will give you the tools you need to get organized.

In the world of accounting, lack of structure means lack of organization, which results in missing important dates and deadlines, often with very serious ramifications. What would your employees do if you missed their direct deposit deadline week after week? They would go work for someone else! No matter how understanding and caring of a leader you are, if you don't stay organized, you are burning your organization down from the inside.

Why Weekly?

Choosing a weekly structure was not a lucky guess or some crazy idea pulled from the sky. To make conscious and accurate business decisions, you need data on a regular and routine basis. Accounting on a weekly basis allows you to look at the minor details of your organization and catch oddities before they become nuclear disasters.

Most small and new businesses live and breathe by cash flow. They often pay employees on a weekly basis to properly manage this cash flow. By looking at sales over cost of goods sold and expenses (such as payroll), you can quickly map a structure through which to learn in-depth about your business.

A weekly structure also makes sense for a less profound reason—we think in days. We plan our weeks around which night we will cook in or go out to eat. We plan our weeks around which days the kids are going to what practice. We plan our life around weeks. Thinking in terms of business, if someone said to do cash deposits on the third Tuesday of the month, why wait to put cash into the bank for almost 30 days? That is asking for a disaster situation and an inability to pay the bills.

Now if I said you need to deposit cash weekly, the wheels in your head start turning. You may say to yourself, *well, my daughter's softball practice is Thursday evening at 6—the bank is on the way, why not stop then*? Now instead of creating a complex schedule that makes your life more challenging, we have created a schedule that fits into your realm of routines. Perhaps you do not have kids but you always have lunch around the same shopping area on Saturday. I guarantee that you will find one bank open on Saturday, or your banks will allow for an overnight deposit. Either way, you can deposit the cash on the way to your favorite lunch spot without worrying about compromising your life or not accomplishing the task on a weekly basis.

Here is an Example

A few years ago I ran an organization with 70 employees and a few million dollars in revenue. We did not have a complex accounting staff or much above the level of QuickBooks Pro in our toolkit. What led us down the road to success, you may ask? A clear and concise weekly schedule that ensured all deposits were made and reporting correct.

Here is a version of that schedule:

Monday
- Check mail, record all deposits and invoices received.
- Record sales from previous week (Tuesday until Sunday).
- Update online banking (Tuesday until Friday).*

Tuesday
- Make cash deposits.
- Finish online banking (for Monday).
- Cut checks for the week (mailing out Tuesday will ensure receipt by Friday).

Wednesday
- Review weekly profit and loss statement.
- Hold all staff meetings associated with finance.

Thursday
- Check mail again, record all invoices received.
- Perform weekly payroll run.

Friday
- Resolve any other outstanding items (re-class expenses, follow up on payments, fix any incorrect checks, etc.).

*Saturday and Sunday banking usually do not clear until Tuesday morning.

The above business reflects a retail business, so a certain importance is placed on specific items. Some of the tasks would differ depending on the field your business operates within. For example, those in consulting or services need to invoice clients on a weekly or monthly basis. Scheduling invoices would need to be added to your schedule to ensure that you invoice quickly and receive prompt payment.

What's the Logic?

The above schedule is a great starter for any small business. The key is not as much which days certain items are completed but rather why they were done on those days. Are you updating your banking for a meeting? Are you mailing checks out so they reach your vendor by the end of the week? Tailor the schedule to work for you and your business, just make sure you understand the logic behind it.

The overall goal is to have accurate and true financials. What's the point of holding a weekly staff meeting and discussing your numbers if the numbers are not accurate? If you are discussing the previous week and none of the invoices are in, you are not tracking the expenses of the firm. If your firm has multiple departments, and you are meeting with a department head, but you have not reviewed the expense he is responsible for—what was the point of the meeting? Having the tools you and your staff need to succeed are crucial to the overall success of the company!

When running a small business, you live and die by your numbers. These figures decide if you can make the much needed new hire or reinvest in your infrastructure. If your numbers are not updated on a weekly basis so you can take a look at weekly financials, then what is the point of the numbers?

As a business owner, you will often have a long-term plan and a short-term plan. These plans will likely have monetary goals attached to them. By setting budget, expenses, or other operating margins against these timelines, you can see if you are succeeding or failing. Don't walk into your meetings empty handed. Ensure you follow a weekly routine so your numbers are prepared and ready to help you make the best possible decision, because at the end of the day that is your job.

Chapter 8

Reconcile Your Domicile

What Is Reconciling?

In layman's terms, reconciling means providing verification that an account balance is correct. For example, we reconcile the balance in the checking account to the balance shown on the bank statement. The objective is to report the correct amount in your checking account in QuickBooks. By reconciling this account you will ensure that you did not miss that crazy bank fee or the receipt from the gas station one employee forgot to turn in.

The Generally Accepted Accounting Principles (GAAP) are a set of accounting principles, procedures, and standards that organizations use in order to compile their financial statements. Generally Accepted Accounting Principles states that the purpose of account reconciliation is to provide accuracy and consistency in financial accounts. To ensure all cash outlays and inlays match between cash flow statements and income statements, it is necessary to carry out reconciliation accounts.

Reconciliation is a process that will benefit your business because it helps avoid errors that may lead to detrimental ramifications. Do you really want to give your business partner a report showing you made money when you didn't? In the world of business, your word is everything. If your financials are based on your word, but those financials are incorrect, well, unfortunately, your word is incorrect.

Reconciliation also plays a valuable role to help against fraud and ensure financial integrity.

Additionally, reconciliations help you spot checks that haven't cleared from months before. Is this vendor still owed money? Was it a duplicated transaction? If so, it needs to be removed, and your financial statements need to be redone. Ultimately, reconciling helps spot errors and ensure you fix them in a timely fashion.

Why Worry About This Reconciling Thing?

Reconciling your books is like taking a test in school. Everyone hates it no matter how good of a student they are. Tests are designed to determine if you mastered the materials that have been studied in the previous period. Like tests, reconciling analyzes your QuickBooks entries to ensure they previous period represents a true and accurate financial picture. We will get into the intricate details of reconciling in this chapter, but more importantly, you need to understand the importance of reconciling.

As you become more experienced within QuickBooks, you may come to find making sales entries and paying bills is a fun and exciting activity. You will use this information to make business decisions and move your enterprise forward. How does one ensure that the information on hand is correct? That is where reconciling comes in—it ensures that all the transactions in your reports are correct and true to form.

Reconciling helps you spot inconsistencies in your books. Perhaps you worked all week and then came home and made some late night transactions in QuickBooks on Friday evening. At the end of the month you will reconcile these transactions and catch that late night mistake you made! Reconciling ensures that errors don't go on for months and years but are resolved within a few weeks.

Additionally, reconciling plays a key role in ensuring that all your money is where it is supposed to be. For example, perhaps you take credit card payments on your tablet or deposit cash weekly at the bank. Oftentimes your credit card processor forgets to batch your money, and sometimes your bank forgets to apply deposits to your account. Crazy as it might sound, it happens all the time—to the tune of hundreds of thousands of dollars. I have seen it firsthand—reconciling ensures that those errors are caught well before you need the money.

Before You Reconcile

Before you reconcile your accounts, check these things:

Be sure you're up-to-date on entering your transactions in QuickBooks. You know that check you wrote last week for your rent but didn't enter in

QuickBooks, or the bills you paid but haven't marked them as paid in QuickBooks? Do that now. Enter all transactions that haven't cleared or shown up on previous bank statements.

The very first time you reconcile, check the Opening Balance transaction on your bank accounts in your QuickBooks Chart of Accounts. They should reflect the amount that was actually in your account when you began using QuickBooks. If it doesn't match, you can fix this by following the below steps:

In your QuickBooks Chart of Accounts, open the register for the account (double-click the account name) and change the Opening Balance transaction to match the ending balance from the last bank statement you received before you started using QuickBooks.

More importantly, you must have all your ducks in a row. Have your statements printed, a coffee, your pen, and a comfy chair. The first time you do this will be challenging, but I promise it gets easier from here.

How Do I Reconcile?

QuickBooks Online

QuickBooks Online makes reconciliations a breeze. First, you must navigate to the Reconcile menu. To do this, simply start at the home screen, click on the

Gear menu, and beneath the column heading Tools, select the Reconcile tab.

The next step is probably your most important—which account will you reconcile? It is important to reconcile all the accounts that I highlight in this chapter. Depending on how your business is set up, it is most beneficial to reconcile receivable, cash on hand, and credit cards prior to your bank account. This helps ensure you track complex errors before doing your bank reconciliation, so you do not have to redo it. Choose the account you want to reconcile from the drop-down menu options (all the accounts are explained below). Once you've selected your account, click Reconcile Now.

Now you must enter your statement details. For bank statements, you just need to enter the end date and ending amount. For items like receivables, cash on hand, etc. you can enter $0 or the actual ending amount. Let's say you have $400 in the cash register draw, that should be your beginning or ending balance. You could also pretend like the $400 does not exist and count based off of $0 for the beginning and ending.

Now the real work begins. Take another look at the transaction history on your bank statement. In the Reconcile window, match each transaction from your bank statement with an item in the list, checking the box to the right of each transaction to match. If you are reconciling other accounts like receivables, just ensure that your outflows match your inflows. For example, if you booked $1,000 in sale on the 5th, you should see that deposit on the 8th.

Now you can finish your reconciliation. When you've gotten the difference value at the bottom to zero you are all set. Though it is important to understand you just don't want a zero ending balance, but rather you want all your transactions that are checked to match those on your statement with a zero ending balance. Clearing transactions for next month while working on last month's bank statements makes no sense!

QuickBooks Desktop (all versions)

QuickBooks Desktop makes reconciliation a bit more challenging, or just more unfriendly to the eyes. To begin your reconciliation, visit the Banking menu and select Reconcile (this option also exists on the home screen, that thing that pops up every time you start QuickBooks).

You will then be prompted to select which account you would like to reconcile, as we discussed above. As indicated above, you enter your account's ending balance in the ending balance section along with the ending date. Then you click continue to begin the reconciliation.

Then check items as they appear on your bank account statement. As you work down the bank statement, your different amount should approach zero, and when your difference is zero, congrats! You can click Reconcile Now, and the reconciliation is complete.

What Exactly Should I Reconcile?

Below is a list of all the accounts you should reconcile and a short background on why they are important.

Bank Account

As you are beginning to realize, reconciling is of the utmost importance. There are multiple accounts that should be reconciled on a monthly basis to ensure accuracy of your accounting—most importantly, the bank account.

Small businesses live and breathe by cash flow or cash on hand. If no cash is on hand, no bills can be paid. If no bills can be paid, employees can't be paid, new inventory can't be bought, the website shuts down, and so on.

QuickBooks gives you an account balance in the bank account based on the transactions within QuickBooks. When you cut checks, hopefully you cut checks so that the balance does not fall below zero. If you have payroll or a tax liability due in the near future, you need to ensure that the checks you cut now and the future payables, combined, do not fall below the dreaded zero mark. Reconciling your bank account ensures that the numbers you base your decisions on are actually accurate.

Some of you may have multiple bank accounts. For example, you could have a payroll clearing account, sales tax liability account, multiple checking accounts for various locations, and so on. Reconciling all bank accounts where money is held should be your number one priority on a monthly basis.

Reconciling your bank accounts also serves an additional purchase rarely mentioned. Reconciling these accounts on a regular basis ensures you are protected from fraud. Fraud of all types occurs in the world of business. Perhaps someone got ahold of a check or your debit card. By reconciling your account on a regular basis you protect yourself from having these transactions go unnoticed. By being aware of these occurrences, you can react in a timely fashion by canceling cards or transferring to a new account with new bank account numbers.

Credit Cards

Liabilities, liabilities, liabilities: They are the root of small business failure. Leverage and debt are great for growing your small business as they allow you to use less of your own capital to get outsized returns. These liabilities are often due on a monthly basis, and this means the outstanding balance must be correct before your payment is due.

Oftentimes, small businesses will give all their employees credit cards because these employees wear many hats—often running to the post office, entertaining a client, making an online purchase, etc. It is vital to ensure that each credit card is reconciled and that there are no nasty surprises hidden away. You want to know in advance if an employee went Christmas shopping on your card!

As mentioned previously, fraud is a major issue when it comes to credit cards, so by ensuring the credit card balances are correct, you ensure that your business metrics are correct. By reconciling your account, you are positive that the charges are correct, and when any surprises arise, you can find out the root of the charge.

Receivables

Perhaps you accept credit cards for your business, or maybe you have a payment processor that deposits every few days. This is considered a receivable, and you want to ensure that you receive all the money that is rightfully yours when you are supposed to.

Booking accurate sales in your system is very important but only half the battle. More important than booking the correct sale is ensuring you get your money. A simple receivable reconciliation can be performed on a weekly or monthly basis.

Oftentimes credit card processors or POS systems hold back money or don't deposit the correct amount. It is your job as the business owner to ensure all the right amounts are deposited. I have occasionally seen processors simply forget to make deposits or hold back money for some wild reason that takes faxing over paperwork to resolve. Either way, by reconciling your receivables you can ensure that you are getting all the money that is rightfully yours.

Payables

Like the many other accounts that need to be reconciled, you must ensure that your payables number matches that of your payables on your balance sheet. This can be a bit confusing at first, but overall you want the bills you have to pay to be showing up properly in your accounts payable.

Before closing the books at the end of each reporting period, you must verify that the detailed total of all accounts payable outstanding matches the payables account balance stated in the general ledger. Doing so ensures that the amount of accounts payable reported in the balance sheet is correct. This is called an accounts payable reconciliation.

This reconciliation process can be a difficult one when performed for the first time. However, once all errors have been spotted and corrections made, it is usually relatively easy to update the reconciliation document in subsequent reporting periods.

Cash on Hand

The hard cash that you have in your possession or sitting around the office, is very important and is referred to as petty cash or cash on hand. You oftentimes pay small bills out of this, or large ones if you frequently deal in cash. These are all business expenses, and it is your job to track these transactions. That is where reconciling cash on hand comes in, allowing you to ensure that all your cash expenditures are accounted for.

Let's say you start the period with $500 in cash on hand locked away in your safe. At the end of the month you count the safe and only have $405 left. It is recommended that you have a place for your receipts or trade receipts for dollars throughout the month. Either way, you should count up those receipts and ensure they match the missing $95. QuickBooks allows you to track all those transactions, and you should. All the receipts should be entered and use the cash on hand bank as the method of purchase.

Now what if you don't have all the receipts of your missing $100? This is a prime example as to why you reconcile often and ensure everything is accounted for. Perhaps your employee ran to the store to get office supplies and forgot to give you the receipt. Or worst-case scenario, perhaps someone in the office has sticky fingers—you need to figure out who it is and how handle it, because $100 can quickly turn into $500.

Fixing Broken Reconciliations

There will be times when you will have worked diligently to update your QuickBooks—adding all the transactions, writing checks out of the system, matching everything to the correct general ledger code—but can't seem to make your reconciliations work.

Well, here are a few potential reasons your reconciliations are broken:

1. You changed something in a previous period that affects a current reconciliation
2. You are missing transactions from a current reconciliation that needs to be added in
3. You entered transactions or wrote checks from the wrong account in QuickBooks

To resolve a previous period issue

Compare the ending account balance in the general ledger for the immediately preceding period to the starting amount in your reconciliation window. Do they match? If these numbers do not match, you will have to reconcile earlier periods before attempting to reconcile the current period.

QuickBooks has a feature called 'Locate Discrepancies.' This should help you find the transaction that was changed, deleted, or added. Take a look at the report and see if the transactions remind you of a previous transaction that exists, does not exist or may have been entered multiple times.

For beginners, it might be best, if it is a recent reconciliation, to undo your previous reconciliation and redo it. Yes, it's a bit more work, but don't you want your books to be accurate? Ideally, after you redo the reconciliation and add or remove the culprit your reconciliation will be ready to go for the current period.

To resolve the issue of missing transactions

Oftentimes we get busy throughout the month and forget to add a debit we made at the gas station or sales from a certain day. This is normal and happens to the best of us—it is the reason why we reconcile.

You will want to go through your reconciliations, for example with the bank statement, circling items that are missing from your QuickBooks. Then, once you get to the end of the reconciliation using the Find feature in QuickBooks Desktop (Edit » Find) or the search bar in QuickBooks Online, you will want to search for those missing amounts. Maybe you entered them but entered them incorrectly. Perhaps you used the checking account but accidentally said you used cash on hand or vice versa.

If you are out of luck and the transactions are nowhere to be found, then it is likely you missed entering them, so go to your check register and enter the missing transactions. Now when you reopen your reconciliation window those transactions will be there for you to match to your statements, bringing your totals right where they need to be!

To resolve the issue of transactions from the wrong account

We mentioned this a bit earlier, but sometimes when you're in a hurry you may write checks, make deposits, or enter expenses within QuickBooks incorrectly. All this means is that you selected the wrong drop-down when performing a certain activity like one mentioned above. For example, did you enter a checking account expense into your savings account?

To resolve this issue, simply revisit the individual transactions. QuickBooks is great because it has drop-down features that let you select which account you would like to print the check from. If you accidentally selected savings but meant checking, simply select the other account from the drop-down.

If you entered expenses in the wrong account, they are likely located in the wrong register. Simply delete these transactions and reenter them in the correct account. When you reconcile at the end of the month, you know you performed it correctly when everything matches!

Chapter 9

Monthly Close

What Exactly Are You Closing—A Door?

Closing the month is a phrase you've definitely heard before. What in the world does it mean? Why are accountants always so busy the first week of the month? What in the world is going on?

Financial reporting is a valuable tool for all businesses because it helps leaders make sound decisions, and sound decisions move businesses forward. To make strong and confident financial decisions, one must have solid financials to base those decisions on.

The monthly closing process ensures that the books for the previous month are accurate and representative of the business. We will go over a mini checklist, but first you must understand that if you do not have a repetitive proven process to close the books, your financials will be inaccurate.

What Should I Do?

Below is a list of items that need to take place to properly close the month. This list is in no particular order and you should order your list in a way that best suits your business.

Close Posting Periods

After you ensure that all your payables and receivables have been recorded for the period, you should consider the period closed. That means you have entered and sent out all the invoices you are aware of for the period. This should really happen within the first week of the following month. Sometimes you will get invoices for the previous period after the period has been closed, simply date them the date of the current month and denote in the memo the correct invoice date. Why? Because the previous period is now closed to all payables entries! If you send out financial statements and then continue to add payables and receivables, then the statements you sent out are inaccurate.

Bank Reconciliation

We went into detail earlier about reconciliations, and now you know that to ensure your financials are accurate and true you must reconcile your bank account. So obviously this is part of the closing process and should be done as soon as everything is entered and you have access to your statement.

Loan & Credit Card Reconciliations

All loan amounts on your balance sheet should tie to your most recent statements. If you owe $100,000 at the end of last month, the balance sheet should say the same amount for that date. Credit cards, also a form of loan, should have all their information entered and then reconciled.

Pro Tip

Credit card reconciliations can sometimes be difficult because their cycles do not fall at the end of the month. The best course of policy is to print your most recent transactions, from let's say the 20th to the end of the month, and reconcile these transactions via the Reconciliation Center of QuickBooks. Do not close the reconciliation! Just ensure all the transactions are entered so your financial statement is accurate.

Tie Out Sales

Oftentimes QuickBooks will serve as a backup for your POS system or your sales staff. To ensure the information is accurate in the accounting software you should reconcile it against any other record you have for recording sales. For example, if you run a retail shop, you should take your sales report from your POS for the previous month and ensure the sales information is exactly the same in QuickBooks. If you run an ecommerce store, you should take your sales reports from your website. If it isn't the same, you must investigate and resolve the discrepancy!

Other Accounts Reconciliation

Let's say you process credit cards through an outside service and you get money every third day. Hopefully you have set up another receivable account to track this money and ensure you are getting all of it. At the end of every month, accounts like this should be reconciled to ensure they are correct.

The same could be said about items like cash on hand. You want to ensure all your expenditures are true and accurate. If the account does not reconcile, figure out where the cash went. if it was used for a purchase, make sure to record those receipts.

Line Item Review

You should know your business inside and out. To ensure that everything is correct and accurate, you should do an in-depth review of your balance sheet and profit and loss statement. Pull these reports within the QuickBooks software and review each line item. Do these income items belong here? Do these expenses belong here? Is this fuel charge for the company vehicle or for the monthly utility at the warehouse? This is a very important step in the financial preparation and monthly close process. Making sure everything is accurate and true at this step will result in fewer headaches down the road.

Not sure how to class something? Well make sure to shoot your CPA an email because a good CPA knows that helping you now will make his or her life easier in March.

The review should not stop at ensuring each item is classified correctly but should also ensure items are in the correct period. At the end of the month are all the invoices truly for that period? You do not want to have your previous month look horrible and current month look great if that is just not true. Proper accounting should flush out large variances unless that is the nature of your business.

Prepare Financials

Once you are confident with all the transactions across the period you can prepare financial statements. Usually this report is prepared for the previous financial month. It includes the profit and loss statement, balance sheet, and cash flow statement.

Management Review

A good leader ensures that everyone is on the same page. The management review of financials also ensures things just aren't out of whack. By reviewing financials with the manager you can ensure that invoices were not slipped by and paid when they shouldn't have been. This ensures that the correct vendors are coded correctly and is a great opportunity to get your management team involved.

Close the Period

The last and probably most important step in the monthly close process is ensuring that no one makes changes to the agreed upon financials after they have been modified for the last time. To do this, simply close the accounting period. This is a simple option in the QuickBooks Desktop under Settings and for QBO users under the Advanced Settings under Company Settings. The period close date should be set to the last day of the previous month, and a password should be set. Generate that password and save it somewhere, but don't share it with your team! If this password is shared with your team then they can make changes to previous periods where you may have already presented financials.

Create a Checklist!

Every company is different and has different financial needs. The reality is the above checklist may not be inclusive of everything you need to close your month or may have offered a list that is too in-depth. Only you will know what is right for your business and should consult with your CPA if you are not quite sure.

The smoothest way to ensure you cover all the necessary items mentioned above is to create a simple checklist in Excel. Create a checklist with which you start fresh every month, with a section for notes. In the hurry of getting the books closed, you may have forgotten to do something or need to make a change the following month. By reviewing the old checklist prior to the current one you will ensure that issues do not plague you up until it is time to file taxes and are instead handled in a timely fashion.

How Should I Organize My Month Close?

If you are a stickler for organization, it is recommended that you find a digital place to house all your information. Perhaps place the files on your computer that you backup regularly, a cloud-based storage service, or an external hard drive. This device or service should be organized by year and then month. All your items for, say, June should be stored within that June folder.

With this organization it will be easier to report to investor, share with your accountant and/ or business partners. Everything will be closed properly and any changes you made will be backed up.

Included in this hub should be everything that you marked off the previously mentioned checklist. Everything from your POS reports to your reconciliation of loans. Don't stop there though, include all your loan statements, bank statements, and anything else pertaining to the month. In the world of accounting and keeping a trail, more is always better!

Chapter 10

Day-to-Day – Properly Perform Simple Daily Tasks

What Have We Missed?

One of the most challenging parts of the accounting aspect for your small business will be the day-to-day tasks that must be accomplished. This list is long and challenging, but do not fret—you will likely only be using a small part of it.

What Are Customers?

Who are your customers? That is the first step you need to ask yourself. For the purpose of simplifying your books, you should look at customers a bit differently than everyone else. In general customers are put into two buckets—flow average sales price with large volume, and high average sales price with low volume. Those categories are distinctively different and should be treated as such.

Low Volume Sellers

If you have a low volume of customers, you want to add a unique customer for each individual or entity you sell to. You may sell to Company A, Company B, and Company C. You may sell to Large Customer 1, Large Customer 2, and Large Customer 3. Each of these is a different customer group and should be set up separately and invoiced individually.

High Volume Sellers

If you have a high volume of customers you should not be tracking every sale individually in QuickBooks. You should track sales by revenue processor. For example, if you have a small online store, you should track sales by your payment processor. An example name is Bank A. If you process through multiple banks or multiple processors, you should have Bank A and Bank B or Processor A and Processor B.

What Are Vendors?

Perhaps you are a vendor and know what this means. Or perhaps you buy from multiple vendors every day. Vendors are those who supply goods and services to you. For example, the tee shirts on the rack that you buy from your friend overseas are purchased from your friend the vendor. The nice lady that comes and cleans the office weekly, yes, she too is a vendor. Each check written to this individual or to these firms should be tracked, which allows you to run vendor reports for a specific time.

How Do I Add and Edit Vendors?

This varies a bit depending on which QuickBooks
version you are using. On the desktop versions, you
will find this feature on the top navigation bar under
Vendors. Once you select the Vendor drop-down,
you can either add a new vendor on the drop-down
or within the Vendor Center. Remember to add all
the necessary information from the tax id to the
address, because when you print checks, this will be
the address that appears on the printed check!

When you utilize QuickBooks Online, the Vendor
option will be on the left side. After you select this,
you will see a button on the top right where you can
select the New Vendor option. Once you add this, a
window will prompt you to enter all the necessary
information as mentioned in the above paragraph.

We will cover coding bank feeds shortly, but once you get all your key vendors set up with the correct name, mailing address, and payment terms, entering bills and coding your bank feeds will be a breeze because everything you need to know about the vendor is right there!

How Do I Enter Bills?

This process will show you how to get bills entered into the QuickBooks accounting software. Obviously this varies a bit between versions, but the core concepts are the same.

If you are using QuickBooks Desktop, you have a quick start button on the home screen that allows you to select Enter bills. If you want to be one of the cool kids, simply select Vendors from the top navigation bar and then select Enter Bills. For those using the QuickBooks Online, simply hit the plus button at the top right of the screen and then select Bill under Vendor.

Where it offers you the option to choose Vendor, you will simply start typing the first few words of the vendor as you would in any autofill software. Once the vendor you are looking for populates, select that one (if it does not yet exist in the system, feel free to add a new vendor).

The next step is what separates the children from the adults. Enter the information from the statement—

invoice number, amount due—and then code the invoice. This is where it can get confusing because you want to ensure your invoice is coded correctly so your financials are correct. Let's say you run a retail shop and buy paper. This paper is used for both the shop printers and the office that services your online business. You are meticulous about where your money goes and want to track the two. So you code each of those paper purchases to "office supplies – office" or "office supplies – retail." Make sure your invoice total matches your entered total, and you coded each purchase to the right general ledger code.

If you set up the correct terms and due date, now when you enter the bills, your cash management will be better in the future. This ensures that when you run payables reports the money and dates you owe vendors will be correct. Remembering the small steps now can save you lots of time in the future.

What Are Checks?

A check is a written, dated, and signed instrument used to make or receive payment. This paper instructs the bank to pay a definite sum of money to a specific individual. For your QuickBooks purposes, you should have checks that can be printed and handwritten checks as well. As you write or print these checks, you should be record them within the QuickBooks system.

How Do I Write Checks?

Automating the check writing process will blow your mind if you have not yet done so. The first step in the process is, as we outlined above, entering Bills section in QuickBooks. Once you successfully complete this process you can move on to writing checks.

The second step in this process after entering your bills is selecting the Pay Bills option. This is located on the home screen on QuickBooks Desktop (or under Vendors and Pay Bills) or under the plus button on QuickBooks Online. In this area you can select which bills you would like paid by simply selecting them—you can even search by vendor of choice.

After you select the bills you would like to pay, either select Pay and Print if using QBO, or Print Later if using QuickBooks Desktop. These transactions have been entered into the system and will adjust your banking balance, but have yet to be printed.

The third and final step in the check-cutting process is printing these checks. This is located on the home screen for QuickBooks Desktop as Print Checks (or under Vendor and Print Checks) or under the plus sign as Vendor Print Checks in QBO. Simply select the checks you would like to print and enter the starting check number (checks should always go in numerical order).

What are Bank Feeds?

Bank feeds are simply the transactions that hit your bank account. This is a great feature of the new accounting software that make the month close process much easier and ensure that all your transactions are properly accounted for (no more double entering transactions or missing a debit charge). These bank transactions appear and allow you to code them as expenses to the correct vendor and associated account.

How to Set Up Bank Feeds?

For QuickBooks desktop users, it is simpler and more cost effective to download your feed from the bank and then upload it into your desktop program. Banks vary in how they let you access this information but you simply want to download the QBO or QBX file for a specified date range and upload into one of the QuickBooks desktop versions.

Once you have this file saved on your computer, you simply go to the Banking drop-down at the top of your program and select Import Bank Feeds. This is a simple and quick way to get all the data from your bank inside the accounting program. The first time you set this up you will have to map the bank you imported to the bank on your balance sheet. So make sure you upload the transactions to your checking if it is your checking or the savings if it is your savings. Once you map or select the right account, QuickBooks Desktop will remember it for future uploads.

For QBO users, the process is a bit different. Under the banking section on the left of your online portal, you should go to the main banking screen. Once there, you can select Add a Bank Account to the banking section. It is a simple process where you simply add your online credentials to the system. Once done, you can map the account to the correct account on the balance sheet. Voila! you will see the bank feeds on your banking section. Instead of manually downloading this information each time, you simply select Update Banking and the banking is updated.

Pro Tip

Bank feeds work for both bank accounts and credit cards. Save time and energy by importing all of these accounts using the QuickBooks built in features.

What Are Bank Feed Rules?

One of the great features of technology is the ability for it to memorize certain actions. QuickBooks bank feeds memorize transactions. For example, do you take your team out for a pizza lunch every Friday? For your convenience, QuickBooks memorizes the name of your pizza place (Pizza Place 1) and the code (meals and entertainment). So every time it sees a transaction from Pizza Place 1 it knows to code it to meals and entertainment.

Pro Tip

Want to figure out your true cash position is for the day? Make sure you update your banking, then you know your position for today.

Want to know your correct check run for the period? Process your bank feeds and select Print Checks. This ensures that you know if you are overdrawing you account in the check-cutting process.

How to Enter Expenses?

As we covered above, one of the key components to managing and entering your expenses will be your bank feeds. The other key component will be manual entry on your end. Perhaps you have a large expense you plan on making tomorrow and want to ensure your cash position is solid. By manually entering this transaction you can ensure that you cash position sustains that kind of purchase. For QuickBooks Desktop, simply enter the Write Checks window, and this will record the expense. For QBO, select the plus sign and Expenses.

For those who want to take it to the next step, you can actually go within the banking register and make adjustments. For example, from the home screen of QuickBooks Desktop, select Check Register to manually add expenses (this is located under Chart of Accounts and the selected register in QBO).

What Is the Item List?

Items are things you buy or sell. These items can be used to generate invoices that you send customers or even to help you enter bills if you wish to track inventory. Item lists help you better organize your invoices by creating items that you use regularly and setting preset prices as well as descriptions

The items can be mapped to COGS or expenses depending on what you are trying to accomplish.

Take the simple example of a wholesale coffee business. The items can be set for each of the three major blends you sell and the three sizes associated with it. Now your COGS could be broken out by each blend so you know what your true cost is each time you sell coffee!

Also, with the Item List is the 'Other Names' list. This is where your business owners live because business owners are neither customers nor vendors. Use this other names list to cut distribution checks or keep your owners' equity in order.

What Are the Different Item Types?

Service

This refers to a service you provide to a customer. For example, window cleaning would be a service. This has no tangible transaction, no goods leave one company and go to another company. In other words, you will have no change in your current inventory. The service item type is great for creating services that you can charge by the job or the hour.

Inventory Part

This refers to an item that you purchase with the goal of reselling. An example of this would be a widget. You bought the widget for $5 and will sell it for $15.

You want to track this item on your balance sheet and book the COGS when the item sells.

Non-Inventory Part

This is an item that is an inventory piece, but one that you do not wish to track with the QuickBooks program.

Other Charge

Here you would add an item like shipping charge, markups, or other items you would like to appear on invoices.

What Are Sales Receipts?

A sales receipt records a sales and the transfer of money, while an invoice is a receivable to be paid. Oftentimes sales receipts are preferred in situations where a POS is not present, and you want payment to occur on the spot. For example, a customer walks in your shop and wants to buy your artwork. Obviously you won't invoice this brand new customer and hope they pay at a later date. You will bill them now, receive the money, record the sale, and then let them walk out the door with the artwork.

For more complex accounting purposes, sales receipts are also great because they record sales for an entire day when you do not want to enter individual transactions. Did your ice cream shop make 150 sales today? Well, obviously you did not want to create a sales receipt for each sale. You can capture all the sales for the day in your POS and transmit this data by simply entering a sales receipt from the information printout from your POS. By entering this sales receipt in QuickBooks, you now have all the financial information you need in your accounting software that was previously in your POS.

How Do I Make Sales Receipts?

For the purpose of most retail and ecommerce businesses, sales receipts will be a blessing. Instead of making complex journal entries, you can simply open the house vendor you created, such as POS Customers, and create a sales receipt to record the sales on a specific day. Oftentimes sales receipts will have line items for refunds, merchant processors, or even different types of product revenues. Tracking these items ensures that your top line revenue is correct and all the associated fees and refunds are recorded.

To set up the sales items, refunds, and processing fees, you simply visit your item list as previously discussed. Here you can create specific items (services are the best because they don't require inventory adjustments). These items help you track sales receipt items so they hit specific line items on your income statement or balance sheet. It is as simple as selecting them when you set up the item!

What Are Sales Journals?

Oftentimes when sales are recorded in another system, such as a Point of Sale, there is a lot of data that needs to be transmitted into QuickBooks. Sales journals help track multiple revenue types with multiple payment processors, allowing you to book complex sales for a given day. Think of a sales journal as a sales receipt on steroids. Instead of going in each customer type, you set up a sales journal to help you organize all of your payment types. For example, if you have multiple profit centers but one payment processor, you want to show on the income statement all the places where the revenue is coming from. Sales journals help you with this process.

How Do I Make a Sales Journal?

Sales journals can get complex quickly, but let's look at a simple journal where you record the sale of goods from your POS. For this example, your POS processes MasterCard and Visa together, separate from American Express. You are going to track your revenue by two revenue types: coffee and ice cream.

4100 - Ice Cream - Credit - $150
4200 - Coffee - Credit - $200
2300 - Sales Tax Payable - Credit $17 (tax rate of 6.5%)
1410 - MasterCard/ Visa Receivable - Debit - $210
1420 - American Express Receivable - Debit - $157

Congrats, you just made your first sales journal! Remember that your debits and credits should also match (equal each other).

Chapter 11

Not Goodbye But A See You Soon

All's Not Lost

Entrepreneurs and small business owners are challenged from all sides the first moment an idea is put into motion. These individuals are truly the Jacks of all trades and the Kings and Queens of wearing many hats. The goal of this book is to make you more confident in wearing the small business accounting hat.

At the beginning of this journey, we covered the basic terminology and chart of accounts. We then went on to the fundamentals and logic of setting up a weekly schedule and properly closing the month. We wrapped up by touching on some key terms and simple concepts such as bank feeds, inputting expenses, and cutting checks.

Overall, you now have the tools you need to get started on your accounting journey or better do what you are already accomplishing. Remember, the key to long term accounting success (and business success) is to *always* ask questions. There are plenty of supplementary accounting resources in addition to this book, and you can always reach out to me directly to get more in-depth guidance. Stay hungry my fellow entrepreneurs.

A toast to your financial success.

About the Author

Zachary Weiner is a full time financial consultant helping small and medium sized startups in the New York area with the financial challenges of growing a business. Partnering with a multitude of companies that are doing cool things, Zac ensures that these pioneers make the right choices so they can be around for the long term.

At the age of 21, Zac partnered with a group of entrepreneurs to change the way online sports lesson transactions occurred. He then went on to lead marketing at a boutique commercial real estate firm out of New York. This lead to his foray into finance and turnaround real estate. Successfully managing a team of nearly 100, Zac turned around multiple distressed real estate properties by stabilizing and allowing for the eventual sale. Heading back to New York, Zac served as the CFO of a growing restaurant group with 15 quick service locations throughout Manhattan and Brooklyn.

Zachary also runs two online accounting services based out of New York and recently published his first e-book (which you just read). In addition to being in the fin-tech space, he also has multiple brands operating on Amazon. It's safe to say he is taking full advantage of the e-commerce wave.

Getting in Touch

If you'd like to know when my next book comes out and want to read similar writing every week, sign up here at www.zacweiner.com for my mailing list. Or follow my boring life on twitter at @zacweiner.

Interested in getting some honest and candid feedback about your business finances? Feel free to email me at zac@zacweiner.com.

If you found anything in this book remotely valuable, there are two ways you could give me a thanks. First, refer this book to a friend who you think will find it beneficial. Secondly, give me heartfelt review on the web or social media.